Original title:
Heartstrings

Copyright © 2024 Swan Charm
All rights reserved.

Author: Daisy Dewi
ISBN HARDBACK: 978-9916-79-215-5
ISBN PAPERBACK: 978-9916-79-216-2
ISBN EBOOK: 978-9916-79-217-9

Invocations of Affection

In whispers soft, we seek the light,
Hearts entwined, in morning's bright.
Each breath we share, a sacred song,
Together, where our souls belong.

With hands held high, we pray and dream,
In love's embrace, we find our theme.
The warmth of grace, a gentle tide,
With faith in love, we shall abide.

Prayer Beads of Shared Experiences

In stories shared, like pearls we string,
Each moment held, a treasured thing.
With laughter woven, pain embraced,
In togetherness, our fears erased.

With every bead, a tale unfolds,
Of joy and sorrow, wisdom bold.
Through timeless bonds, our spirit grows,
In love's vast ocean, true grace flows.

Devoted in Sacred Silence

In quietude, our hearts align,
Silent prayers, in love we find.
A sacred space, where spirits glow,
In peace profound, we come to know.

With reverence, we dwell in trust,
In stillness pure, our souls combust.
Together here, we softly breathe,
In sacred silence, love we weave.

The Light of Companionship

In shadows deep, you hold my hand,
With each warm touch, a promise stands.
The light of you, it guides my way,
In every night, you are my day.

Through trials faced, our bond grows strong,
In unity, we both belong.
The shining grace, our lives entwined,
In love's embrace, our hearts aligned.

The Blessings of Synchronicity

In whispers of fate, we find our way,
Guided by light, through night and day.
Moments collide, as stars align,
In the sacred dance of the divine.

Each glance, each sign, a thread of grace,
Carving a path, in time and space.
Hand in hand, we share this gift,
Our spirits soar, in love we lift.

Sanctified Strings of Togetherness

In unity we gather, hearts entwined,
With every heartbeat, a truth defined.
Sanctified souls, a chorus strong,
Together we rise, where we belong.

Threads of compassion weave our fate,
Binding our lives, we celebrate.
In the tapestry of faith we find,
A sacred bond, eternally aligned.

The Love That Moves the Heavens

Through every trial, love's light flows,
In the darkest nights, a flame still glows.
With hearts ablaze, we reach for the sky,
In love's embrace, we learn to fly.

Moments of silence, whispers of prayer,
In the stillness, we feel Him there.
The world transforms, through love's embrace,
Heaven extends, in time and space.

Footsteps on the Divine Path

With humble hearts, we seek the way,
In every footstep, the truth will stay.
Guided by faith, we tread with care,
The path is sacred, a promise rare.

Each challenge faced, a lesson learned,
In the fire of life, our souls are burned.
Yet hand in hand, we bravely walk,
In the quiet moments, we hear Him talk.

An Offering of Linked Spirits

In the stillness of the night,
Whispers rise, a sacred plight.
Hearts entwined in fervent prayer,
Souls alight, embracing the air.

With hands uplifted to the skies,
We seek the truth that never lies.
Together, walking on this path,
In faith, we cast aside our wrath.

The echoes of our sacred song,
Where love and grace do both belong.
With every breath, we share this call,
In unity, we rise, we fall.

Through trials faced, we find our way,
In light of dawn, we choose to stay.
An offering of linked spirits strong,
In harmony, we shall belong.

In silence, with the stars above,
We recognize the power of love.
Each heartbeat sings a melody,
Divine connection, we are free.

Divine Resonance of Affections

In quietude, our spirits blend,
A symphony where souls transcend.
With each tender glance we share,
The universe breathes love and care.

Waves of joy wash over me,
In the stillness, our hearts decree.
A resonance that binds us tight,
In every shadow, seeking light.

With every prayer, we lift our gaze,
To honor love in wondrous ways.
Together, weaving threads so fine,
A tapestry of heart entwined.

In the laughter, in the tears,
We find the peace that calms our fears.
Through every heartbeat, every sigh,
Affections soar into the sky.

Divine whispers in the night's embrace,
Guiding us to a sacred place.
In shared silence, promises made,
Love's eternal grace displayed.

The Language of Graceful Bonds

Words unspoken, hearts align,
In gentle touch, our spirits shine.
The language flows like rivers wide,
In unity, we do abide.

Through trials shared and joys embraced,
In life's tapestry, we are laced.
Each moment cherished, pure and true,
In every heartbeat, me and you.

With every breath, a hymn we sing,
In every dawn, new hope we bring.
A bond transcending time and space,
In love, we find our sacred place.

Through storms that test our fragile hearts,
We stand together, never parts.
Connected by a thread so fine,
Divine love flows, forever thine.

In whispered prayers and dreams confined,
A graceful bond, so rare to find.
Together, let our spirits soar,
In the language of love, forevermore.

Divine Threads of Emotion

In the fabric of our hearts,
Woven dreams and sacred arts.
Threads of emotion, tight and strong,
In unity, we all belong.

With each heartbeat, stories told,
In silent prayers, our hopes unfold.
The tapestry of love we weave,
In faith, together we believe.

Through the shadows, light will break,
In every smile, the choice we make.
Each moment stitched with care and grace,
A divine connection we embrace.

With threads of joy, and strands of sorrow,
We find the strength to face tomorrow.
In gentle whispers, faith is sewn,
In this sacred bond, we are not alone.

In the warmth of love's embrace,
We know the beauty of this space.
Divine threads of emotion stand,
Intertwined by a loving hand.

Ethereal Ties of Devotion

In the quiet of the night,
Whispers of love take flight.
Hearts entwined in sacred grace,
Finding peace in Your embrace.

Hands raised high in reverent air,
Seeking comfort in Your care.
Every prayer a silent plea,
Binding souls eternally.

In the light of morning's glow,
Devotion deepens, spirits flow.
Like rivers running pure and wide,
In Your presence, we confide.

Through trials faced and shadows cast,
Your light guides us through the vast.
With faith, our burdens we shed,
Walking onward where You've led.

As stars align in celestial dance,
We surrender to Your trance.
With hearts ablaze, we pledge our troth,
In the bond of love, we've growth.

The Chapel of Our Union

Within these walls, our hearts unite,
In sacred space, all feels right.
Fingers interlaced in prayer,
Echoes of love fill the air.

Candles flicker, shadows play,
Each moment cherished, night and day.
In this chapel, purest grace,
We find solace in Your face.

The altar bright with every vow,
In front of You, we humbly bow.
With every whisper, every song,
In this union, we belong.

Let the world fade far away,
As we bask in love's soft sway.
In this hallowed, holy place,
We discover our saving grace.

When storms arise and shadows loom,
Together, we dispel the gloom.
In this sacred space, we thrive,
Forever in love, we're alive.

Beloved Beneath the Stars

Beneath the night's enchanting dome,
We find solace, our hearts roam.
Stars like candles, burning bright,
Guide us through the velvet night.

Your laughter dances on the breeze,
In Your love, my spirit sees.
Celestial whispers, soft and clear,
In every heartbeat, You are near.

As constellations spin and twirl,
You are my love, my precious pearl.
Even in silence, our souls speak,
In this union, we are complete.

With every glance, our hopes ignite,
Every moment, pure delight.
Hand in hand, through time we'll tread,
In Your light, our fears are shed.

Beloved, in this vast expanse,
Let us embrace this sacred chance.
Together under cosmic light,
Our love, eternal, shines so bright.

Spiritual Latticework of Longing

In the depths of yearning hearts,
A tapestry of love imparts.
Every thread, a whispered dream,
In this lattice, we believe.

As the soul seeks out the flame,
In Your name, we stake our claim.
Through tangled paths and winding ways,
Our unwavering hope still stays.

In the quiet hush of prayer,
We weave our wishes, laid bare.
Each longing tethered to the sky,
Together, we will rise and fly.

With every breath, a promise made,
In faith's embrace, fears start to fade.
Through trials, both near and far,
Your guiding light, our shining star.

Latticework of dreams divine,
In this bond, our spirits intertwine.
With every heartbeat, love is strong,
In every moment, we belong.

Elysian Pursuits of the Heart

In the garden where spirits meet,
Whispers of love dance in the air.
Stars entwined in a sacred beat,
Hearts uplifted, free from despair.

Every prayer a gentle breeze,
Carrying hopes to the divine.
In the stillness, hearts find ease,
Each soul's journey forever twine.

With faith as a guiding light,
We seek the path so true and bright.
In the depths of yearning's night,
Love's embrace ignites our flight.

In celestial halls we roam,
Finding solace in the grace.
Each step leads us closer home,
To the warmth of love's embrace.

Through trials that test our might,
We rise with hearts that never cease.
To the chorus of pure delight,
Elysian dreams grant us peace.

Sonnet of the Celestial Embrace

From distant realms where angels sing,
The tapestry of love is spun.
In every heart, a sacred flame,
Binding souls as bright as the sun.

In shadows cast by doubt and fear,
The light of faith shines ever clear.
With hands entwined, we draw so near,
In silent prayer, our hearts adhere.

Each moment shared, a holy gift,
As spirits soar on wings of grace.
In love's embrace, our hearts do lift,
United in this sacred space.

Together we will brave the storm,
In trials faced, our souls align.
With every touch, love's light is born,
A dance of fate, a grand design.

Eternally, our faith will guide,
Through sacred bonds we find our way.
In love, we flourish, side by side,
In celestial embrace, we stay.

The Altar of Intimate Bonds

Upon the altar where hearts unite,
Vows whispered soft, a sacred trust.
In every glance, pure love ignites,
With gentle hands, we build our just.

The harmony of souls entwined,
Each heartbeat tells a tale so sweet.
In trials met, our love defined,
With every step, our spirits meet.

In silence deep, our thoughts converge,
The sacred space of hopes and dreams.
From depths of faith, pure feelings surge,
Love flourishes, bursting at the seams.

With every prayer, our hearts align,
As angels watch with tender care.
In the embrace of love divine,
We rise above, free from despair.

In timeless bonds, through joy or strife,
Together walk this hallowed ground.
The altar glows with radiant life,
In love's pure grace, we are found.

Serene Ties of Sacred Love

In the stillness of the night,
Whispers of love fill the skies.
Every star, a guiding light,
A testament to hearts that rise.

Every promise a sweet refrain,
Boundless faith in every heart.
Through joy and sorrow, love's true pain,
In sacred ties, we never part.

With gentle hands, we weave our fate,
In harmony, our spirits soar.
Together we create, relate,
Embraced by love forevermore.

In the garden of our sweet dreams,
Where laughter echoes pure and bright,
Serene ties of love confer beams,
A sanctuary filled with light.

Through trials faced, we stand as one,
In faith we find our path of bliss.
With every dawn, a new begun,
In sacred love, sealed with a kiss.

Graceful Intercessions of Love

In quiet whispers, prayers ascend,
Hearts entwined, the souls they mend.
With grace, we seek the divine light,
In love's embrace, we find our right.

Fingers clasped in humble plea,
Together shaping our destiny.
Through trials faced, we each confess,
In unity, we find our blessedness.

Like morning dew on petals fair,
The touch of grace, a sacred air.
From shadows cast, we turn our gaze,
To love's pure glow, through endless days.

In sacred rooms where silence speaks,
We gather strength in gentle tweaks.
With each breath, we lift our aim,
To honor love, the sweetest name.

Through every tear, and joyful shout,
In loving circles, faith doesn't doubt.
In God's embrace, we cast our fears,
Graceful intercessions, through the years.

Scriptorium of Sacred Affection

In the scriptorium of the heart,
Words of love, a sacred art.
Each letter penned with pure intent,
For every moment, ever spent.

By candlelight, we write our dreams,
In ink that flows like sacred streams.
Each verse a testament we scribe,
Of love that gives, and peace describes.

Ancient texts, in whispers found,
Echo through the hallowed ground.
With every word, our spirits rise,
In written truths, we touch the skies.

In fellowship, we share our lore,
Open hearts, forever more.
With sacred stories, love unfolds,
In every page, a bond upholds.

Amongst these tomes, we learn and grow,
The binding force, the sacred flow.
In the scriptorium's hallowed space,
We find our strength, our truest grace.

Illuminated Paths of Togetherness

Upon the hill where shadows play,
We walk together, come what may.
With lanterns bright, our spirits bold,
On illuminated paths, we unfold.

In unity, we face the night,
Hand in hand, we seek the light.
Through trials faced and joys we share,
Together, burden's ease we bear.

With every step, a sacred bond,
In love's embrace, we find our fond.
In laughter sweet and moments rare,
Illuminated paths, we declare.

Through thick and thin, in peace we tread,
With hearts alight, no word left said.
In harmony, our voices blend,
On these paths, we shall transcend.

So let us journey, side by side,
In faith's embrace, our hearts are tied.
For on these illuminated ways,
Together, we sing of brighter days.

Tapestry of Divinity and Desire

Woven strands of love's fine thread,
In every tale, a life is bred.
A tapestry of dreams we weave,
In divine patterns, we believe.

Colors bright, and shadows soft,
Each stitch a prayer, our souls aloft.
In sacred hands, our hearts entwine,
A masterpiece by designs divine.

From silence comes a whispered thread,
In every hope, our spirits spread.
Each moment lived, a fiber strong,
In love's embrace, we truly belong.

With every heartbeat, tales unfold,
In threads of longing, stories told.
Together, we craft our fate,
In divinity, we celebrate.

In the loom of life, we find our way,
A tapestry crafted day by day.
With threads of faith and love's sweet fire,
We gather close, our hearts' desire.

Emissaries of Eternal Affection

In dusk's embrace, soft whispers rise,
Heaven's light beams from the skies.
Hearts united, in faith they soar,
Love transcends, forevermore.

Through trials faced and storms that pass,
Each moment sacred, bubbles like glass.
Hand in hand, the brave shall tread,
With grace and hope, their spirits fed.

Memories woven in prayer's sweet balm,
For in His embrace, we find our calm.
Gentle nudges from realms divine,
Illuminated paths, a sacred sign.

Together as one, we rise and sing,
Joyful echoes in praises ring.
Emissaries of love, bright as day,
In His glory, we find our way.

For love is the thread that ties us tight,
In darkness, we seek the guiding light.
Eternal affection shall not forsake,
United in spirit, for His own sake.

The Blessed Entanglement of Souls

In silence we meet, beneath the stars,
Souls entangled, no distance far.
A whisper of love, a touch divine,
In sacred breath, our hearts align.

Through trials faced, we rise anew,
Each joy shared, each sorrow true.
By faith entwined, we navigate,
Together we shine, never late.

Light we gather from heaven's core,
Reflecting warmth, forevermore.
In gentle eyes, the truths unfold,
Stories of love, eternally told.

Through valleys deep and mountains high,
We walk in grace, you and I.
A bond unbroken, by spirit sealed,
In the tapestry of love, revealed.

In moments fleeting, our hearts explore,
The blessed entanglement, never poor.
In every thread of this holy weave,
We find the strength to ever believe.

The Graced Connection of Hearts

In quiet prayer, our voices blend,
Two hearts as one, love does not end.
The sacred journey forever leads,
In every action, kindness feeds.

Through gentle hands and tender grace,
We find our home in each embrace.
A mirthful laugh, a tearful sigh,
In unity's warmth, we soar and fly.

With every heartbeat, God's echo calls,
In life's great dance, His spirit sprawls.
Connecting souls through time and fate,
In love's true flow, we cultivate.

In storms we stand, through shadows cast,
Together we rise, our fears surpassed.
For love's connection, ever strong,
In the hymn of life, we sing our song.

The graced connection wraps us tight,
In every darkness, we find the light.
With open hearts, we choose to share,
As vessels of love, beyond compare.

A Journey Through Holy Emotions

On this journey, we walk in prayer,
With open hearts, we lay them bare.
Each step a whisper, each breath a song,
In holy emotions where we belong.

Through valleys low and mountains grand,
His guiding light holds our hand.
With every laughter, and every tear,
We find His presence, oh so near.

In the depth of silence, truth is found,
A friendship forged, forever bound.
In the echo of love, our spirits rise,
Through the lens of faith, we reach the skies.

In moments fleeting, we gather grace,
With every heartbeat, we find our place.
Together we navigate, never apart,
A journey of passion, a journey of heart.

Through holy emotions, our souls unite,
In love's embrace, forever bright.
Side by side, we march along,
In this sacred dance, we sing our song.

Revelations of the Intimate

In whispers soft, the truth we find,
A sacred space where hearts align.
Divine presence, gentle and clear,
In the silence, love draws near.

From shadows cast, a light appears,
Guiding us through our hopes and fears.
With every breath, a promise made,
In unity, our doubts will fade.

Together, we walk this holy path,
In joy we dance, in love we bask.
The warmth of grace, a tender kiss,
In every moment, a glimpse of bliss.

Through trials faced, we rise anew,
Bound by faith, steadfast and true.
In echoes deep, the soul takes flight,
In one another, we find the light.

With hearts unveiled, we share the flame,
In every heartbeat, praise your name.
A tapestry of souls we weave,
In divine love, we shall believe.

Celestial Harmonies of Togetherness

In starlit skies, we hear the call,
A symphony where spirits enthrall.
Together we rise, a choir of grace,
In the sacred dance, we find our place.

With hands entwined, we journey far,
Guided by each resplendent star.
In each heartbeat, a sacred song,
In unity's arms, we belong.

The heavens echo our deepest prayers,
In every struggle, love declares.
Through trials faced, our spirits soar,
In sacred bonds, we are much more.

Through storms of life, we stand as one,
In each moment, a love well spun.
With open hearts, we seek, we find,
In celestial harmony, souls entwined.

In stillness, we share dreams unseen,
A bond of faith, a life serene.
We weave our stories, hand in hand,
In love's embrace, together we stand.

Blessings in the Space Between

In the quiet pause, grace does flow,
In every moment, love will grow.
Between the words, a truth resides,
In silent prayer, our spirit guides.

The space between, a hallowed ground,
In every heartbeat, blessings found.
With open hearts, we choose to see,
In stillness, lies our harmony.

Through trials faced, we seek the light,
In every challenge, love ignites.
The whispers soft, the echoes loud,
In unity, we stand so proud.

In each embrace, the world transforms,
In love's embrace, our spirit warms.
With every breath, we rise as one,
In sacred bond, our souls have spun.

In twilight's glow, we linger long,
In every moment, we are strong.
With gratitude, we bless the space,
In love's creation, we find our place.

Everlasting Glimmers of Truth

In valleys deep, where shadows dwell,
The glimmers of truth begin to swell.
A flicker bright in darkest night,
Illuminates paths, brings forth the light.

With every heartbeat, wisdom flows,
In sacred moments, it gently grows.
Like rivers wide, it carves the stone,
Revealing lessons, forever known.

The sun will rise, the dawn will break,
In radiant hues, what truth awakes.
In every glance, in every sigh,
The whispers of time, they never die.

Within the heart, a compass turns,
In every soul, the fire burns.
We hold the keys to realms untold,
Everlasting glimmers, pure and bold.

So seek the light, let shadows fade,
In truth's embrace, we are remade.
For in the journey, we shall find,
The sacred ties that bind mankind.

Echoes of Celestial Love

In every beat, the echoes sound,
A love divine that knows no bound.
Through endless skies, soft whispers flow,
In every heart, this truth we know.

As stars align, and dreams take flight,
The universe sings of love's pure light.
In gentle breezes, we feel the grace,
Of celestial arms in warm embrace.

The moonlit path, a guiding way,
In sacred love, we choose to stay.
With open hearts, we rise above,
In unity found, echoes of love.

Through trials faced and joys proclaimed,
In every moment, love unchained.
As time flows on, its rhythm true,
In every breath, I find you anew.

With gratitude, we walk this road,
In every step, a sacred code.
For love transcends, and always will,
In echoes soft, we hear it still.

Shards of Divine Sunlight

In dawn's embrace, the light descends,
A tapestry where love transcends.
Soft beams awaken the sleeping earth,
In shards of sunlight, we find rebirth.

With every ray, a promise made,
In golden hues, our fears allayed.
The warmth surrounds, in gentle art,
Illuminating the shadowed heart.

In nature's choir, the voice is clear,
A symphony that draws us near.
Each glimmer sparks a hope anew,
In healing light, our spirits grew.

As petals bloom, and rivers flow,
The divine sunlight begins to show.
A sacred dance in each precious dawn,
In every moment, we are reborn.

So raise your gaze, embrace the light,
In shards of sun, we find our sight.
For in this glow, the truth will gleam,
A boundless love, a radiant dream.

The Flame of Hope's Ascent

In shadows deep, the candle's light,
Burns bright with grace, through darkest night.
With whispers soft, the heart does yearn,
As hope ignites, our spirits burn.

The path is steep, yet faith shall guide,
Through valleys low, with love beside.
In trials faced, resilience grows,
The flame of hope, forever glows.

Each prayer a spark, igniting skies,
In fervent faith, our souls arise.
Together strong, we journey on,
For in the light, we find our dawn.

With hands held high, and dreams in sight,
We stand as one, in holy light.
Through every storm, we shall ascend,
In unity, our hearts transcend.

So let us rise, the flame we keep,
A promise made, our hope runs deep.
In every heart, the fire starts,
A tapestry of sacred arts.

Illuminations of the Spirit

In silence deep, the spirit gleams,
Where love resides, and faith redeems.
With gentle whispers, truth unseals,
In every prayer, the heart reveals.

The morning breaks, with light divine,
Our souls awakened, in love's design.
With every breath, the joy we find,
In holy grace, our hearts aligned.

Together we walk, with hands entwined,
Through sacred paths, our lives combined.
The spirit shines, in every face,
Unlocking doors to boundless grace.

With grateful hearts, we rise and sing,
In joyful praise, our voices ring.
The light of love, forever flows,
In every soul, the spirit grows.

Through trials faced, we hold the light,
Our spirits soar, like birds in flight.
In every tear, a lesson learned,
In illuminated hearts, we burn.

So let us dance, in radiant air,
With open hearts, our burdens share.
Illuminations of the spirit bright,
Guide us all to eternal light.

The Soft Glow of Devotion

In quiet moments, hearts align,
With soft glow, divine design.
In daily tasks and evening prayer,
Devotion blooms, in love we share.

Beneath the stars, our spirits sing,
Each whispered hope, a sacred thing.
With every beat, our hearts confess,
In humble grace, we find our rest.

The softest touch, a gentle hand,
In silent faith, together stand.
Through trials faced, our bond remains,
In quiet love, no loss, just gains.

With every dawn, a page anew,
In gratitude, our souls renew.
In every prayer, a chance to grow,
The soft glow brightens, hearts aglow.

Together we tread, this sacred ground,
In faces bright, devotion found.
Through every storm, the light will stay,
In softest glow, we find the way.

So let us cherish, the moments dear,
With every heartbeat, have no fear.
In soft devotion, forever free,
In the light of love, we shall be.

Shining Through Turmoil

In shadows cast, where doubts arise,
A light within, will not disguise.
Through every trial, our spirits fight,
In turmoil's grip, we seek the light.

With steadfast hearts, we stand as one,
Through darkest nights, we greet the sun.
With every prayer, our strength shall grow,
Shining through, we learn to glow.

In mountains high, and valleys low,
Our faith endures, through ebb and flow.
With every tear, a seed is sown,
In trials faced, we're never alone.

Each setback faced, a chance to rise,
In the midst of chaos, hope defies.
With eyes fixed firm, the way is clear,
Together we shine, immersed in cheer.

Through whispered doubts, and heavy sighs,
The spirit lifts, and never lies.
In sacred trust, we hold the key,
To shine through turmoil, wild and free.

So let us stand, with hearts ablaze,
In unity, our voices raise.
For in the dark, love's light shall bloom,
Shining through, we conquer gloom.

Glimmers of Faith

In the silence, whispers breathe,
Hope like candles flicker bright,
Each moment now, a heart believes,
Guided by the sacred light.

Through the storms, we find our way,
Hands uplifted, souls unite,
With every prayer, we choose to stay,
In the embrace of love's delight.

Mountains high, valleys wide,
Faith will carry, hearts will soar,
In the stillness, we confide,
Trusting in the evermore.

The dawn will break with grace anew,
As shadows fade, our spirits rise,
In every breath, a promise true,
Glimmers shine 'neath endless skies.

Together here, in holy space,
We lift our voices, pure and clear,
Faith's warm glow, a sweet embrace,
In the presence of the dear.

The Sacred Illumination

From the depths, a light ascends,
Filling hearts with warmth and bliss,
In the quiet, time suspends,
Each moment wrapped in divine kiss.

A tranquil night, the stars appear,
Voices murmur, songs arise,
In our hearts, we shed the fear,
As the sacred truth complies.

Every path, a choice of grace,
Leading souls to realms above,
With each step, we find our place,
In the rhythm of pure love.

Radiant beams through shadows fall,
Guiding lost, and lifting high,
In the stillness, we hear the call,
Faith's embrace will never die.

Through the trials, hope ignites,
Turning darkness into gold,
In the sacred, inner lights,
Illuminated paths unfold.

Hearts Aglow with Purpose

In the garden, blooms of faith,
Sprouting hope with every prayer,
Hearts alive, with love to wraith,
Every burden we will share.

Songs of joy, in air they flow,
United as the morning dawns,
With each heartbeat, seeds we sow,
Underneath the watchful fawns.

Purpose shines, a guiding star,
Leading souls through life's vast maze,
In our journey, near and far,
Hearts aglow, in love we blaze.

Through the night, we find our way,
In the laughter, in the tears,
Hand in hand, come what may,
Embracing all throughout the years.

Together we will forge our dreams,
In the light of unity's grace,
With every trial, stronger themes,
Hearts aglow, in faith's embrace.

The Divine Illuminator's Embrace

In the shadows, love alights,
Bringing forth the brightest day,
With each heartbeat, sacred rites,
In the stillness, we will stay.

Hearts entwined in blissful grace,
Dancing softly, spirits soar,
In the presence of this space,
We find joy forevermore.

Eyes to heaven, souls unfold,
Yearning for the truth to see,
Every story softly told,
In the light of unity.

In this moment, we are free,
Wrapped in warmth of heaven's glow,
As we share, in harmony,
Love's sweet river's gentle flow.

Through the trials, we embrace,
In the whispers, faith ignites,
In our spirits, find the trace,
Of the Divine, our guiding lights.

Pathways to Radiance

Upon the road where spirits soar,
Guided by light forevermore,
With faith a lantern bright we hold,
In shadows deep, our hearts turned bold.

Each step we take, a prayer in kind,
In every heartbeat, peace we find,
The whispers of the sacred call,
Inviting souls to rise and fall.

Through trials faced and lessons learned,
In every fracture, strength is earned,
The journey carved in trust and grace,
We walk each path, a holy space.

The stars above, a cosmic map,
With every thought, a loving tap,
To draw us closer, hand in hand,
Towards the light, a timeless band.

In unity, our spirits gleam,
Awakening in a shared dream,
Together on this radiant way,
We find the dawn in each new day.

Illuminated Souls

In the silence, hearts ignite,
Radiating warmth, a sacred light,
With every breath, a song we weave,
In love's embrace, we dare believe.

The truth unfolds like petals rare,
In moments shared, we find our care,
Each soul a mirror, reflecting grace,
In unity, we find our place.

Through trials dark, our spirits rise,
Connection binds, a sacred tie,
We lift our voices, a chorus grand,
In the glow of faith, together we stand.

The beauty shines from deep within,
In kindness shared, our lives begin,
Illuminated paths we tread,
With hearts aflame, our fears are shed.

In quietude, we seek the soul,
Embracing love, our ultimate goal,
With every step, a dance divine,
In illuminated light, we shine.

Journey to the Divine Glow

In search of light, we roam afar,
Each step a prayer, our guiding star,
With open hearts, we boldly tread,
On golden paths where angels led.

Through valleys deep and mountains high,
With faith as wings, together we fly,
In quiet moments, the spirit speaks,
Awakening the joy each seeker seeks.

The sacred whispers in the breeze,
Invite us closer to inner peace,
Each journey carved in love and trust,
Transforming dust to stars, we must.

With every challenge, a lesson gains,
In pain, we grow, our spirit trains,
The glow of grace, a beacon bright,
Illuminating pathways in the night.

Together we gather, hands entwined,
In love's embrace, the ties that bind,
Towards the divine, let our hearts go,
A journey led by that sacred glow.

Awakening the Inner Flame

Within the heart, a flame resides,
A spark of love that never hides,
In moments still, let it arise,
Igniting dreams beneath the skies.

Through storms that shake and winds that roar,
We nurture light, it grows, it soars,
With gentle hands, we tend the fire,
Exploring depths, our hearts inspire.

The warmth it brings, a sacred balm,
A whispered song, a gentle calm,
When darkness falls, we stand as one,
To share the light, till day is done.

Awake, O souls, in radiant cheer,
Embrace the flame, let go of fear,
In every heartbeat, courage blooms,
Creating light in shadowed rooms.

The inner flame, a guiding light,
Unites our spirits, ignites the night,
Together we shine, forever free,
Awakening love's eternity.

Blossoming in Sacred Light

In gardens where the angels sing,
Hearts awaken to the spring.
Petals unfurl in holy grace,
Seeking the light, a warm embrace.

Each moment blooms in pure delight,
Guided by the sacred light.
Whispers gently on the breeze,
Nature's hymn brings us to our knees.

In silence, prayers begin to rise,
A fragrant offering to the skies.
With every breath, we feel the call,
To cherish love, to nurture all.

From earth to heaven, dreams take flight,
In faith, we tread a path so bright.
With every step, our spirits soar,
Embracing life, forevermore.

Shadows Transformed to Shine

In twilight's grasp, the sorrows fade,
A promise kept, our hopes displayed.
Through trials deep, the spirit learns,
That from the dark, the candle burns.

With every tear, new strength is born,
In silence, whispers of the morn.
Resilience blooms, a sacred song,
To turn the night to right the wrong.

From shadows cast, our light will rise,
A beacon bright beneath the skies.
In unity, we start to heal,
With every heart, a chance to feel.

As dawn appears, we stand renewed,
In gratitude, our souls imbued.
The light will chase the dark away,
In faith united, come what may.

Treading the Hallowed Path

With humble hearts, we seek the way,
On paths where saints and seekers pray.
Each step we take, a sacred vow,
To honor love, to cherish now.

In every breath, a purpose clear,
The whispers of the Divine draw near.
With open minds, we learn and grow,
Embracing all that we can know.

Through trials faced and joys embraced,
With every moment, His grace traced.
We walk as one, in truth's embrace,
Finding divinity in each place.

As seasons turn, we hold the light,
Guided by faith through day and night.
In harmony, our spirits sing,
On sacred journeys, love takes wing.

Chasing the Eternal Dawn

With every breath, the dawn we chase,
An endless journey through time and space.
Each hope ignited, a flame divine,
In every heart, His love will shine.

When darkness looms and shadows play,
We lift our voices, come what may.
In unity, we cast aside,
The doubts that linger in our stride.

For in the light, our dreams revive,
The spirit's song, forever thrive.
We dance through life with open hands,
In search of grace in distant lands.

With every step, belief imbued,
The dawn is here, our spirits renewed.
Together we rise, in faith we stand,
Chasing the dawn, in hearts so grand.

In Search of Divine Radiance

In valleys deep where shadows lie,
I seek Your light, O Lord on high.
Through whispered prayers, my spirit yearns,
For every heart, Your warmth returns.

The gentle breeze, a sacred song,
Guides me, Lord, where I belong.
With every tear, a grace unfolds,
In faith, Your truth my heart upholds.

With open hands, I stand to greet,
The dawn that comes, pure and sweet.
Your love, a beam that fills the air,
In silent moments, I find You there.

Through trials fierce and grief so vast,
Your presence shines, a light amassed.
In every doubt, You calm my soul,
With You, my heart becomes made whole.

O radiant One, my spirit sings,
In search of You, my heart takes wings.
Forevermore, my life I'll share,
In search of love beyond compare.

The Sacred Illumination

In shadows cast by mortal strife,
Your light emerges, granting life.
A whisper soft, a gentle call,
O sacred flame, You guide us all.

Through every prayer from hearts that yearn,
Your love ignites, and souls discern.
With open hearts, we seek to find,
The path that brings the lost to mind.

In every dawn, Your grace descends,
Inviting peace as daylight bends.
Above the storm, Your presence glows,
A beacon bright, our spirit knows.

The sacred word, a light revealed,
In every heart, Your truth is sealed.
With every breath, Your love abounds,
In sacred moments, grace surrounds.

Though trials test and fears may rise,
We lift our hearts toward endless skies.
For in Your light, we find our way,
Through deepest night and brightest day.

Abiding in the Divine Dawn

As morning breaks, the world anew,
Your love unfolds in every hue.
With each soft ray, I seek to see,
The sacred truth that sets me free.

In silence pure, my heart takes flight,
To gather strength from holy light.
O Divine dawn, Your presence clear,
With every breath, I draw You near.

Through whispered prayers, my spirit wakes,
In sacred moments, stillness takes.
Your mercy flows, a gentle stream,
Where hope ignites, and hearts redeem.

In every trial, my faith will stand,
With open heart and outstretched hand.
O abiding light, forever true,
In every dawn, I dwell with You.

As shadows fade and fears recede,
Your love comforts, it's all I need.
In grace, I walk, with You beside,
Abiding in the Divine's wide tide.

Revelations in Soft Glimmers

In sacred night beneath the stars,
Your wisdom shines, erasing scars.
With every glance, new truths emerge,
In gentle whispers, hearts converge.

The quiet light reveals the way,
In soft glimmers, my soul will stay.
Through trials faced and shadows cast,
Your love upholds, steadfast and vast.

In moments brief, the heart takes flight,
Revelations spark in darkest night.
With each soft glimmer, I behold,
A dance of faith, a flame of gold.

Your presence felt in every sigh,
Through gentle grace, You draw me nigh.
In sacred glimmers, truth unfolds,
A tapestry of love retold.

O wondrous light, forever shine,
In every heart, Your love divine.
In soft revelations, spirits blend,
Transforming lives, our hearts transcend.

Guided by Holy Whispers

In silence deep, His voice is clear,
Whispers of love, a gentle cheer.
Through shadows cast, His light shall grace,
Guiding us all to a sacred place.

In storms of doubt, we seek the way,
With faith our shield, we shall not sway.
Each whispered prayer, a soft embrace,
Carried on winds, to Heaven's space.

From hearts ablaze, His truth is sung,
In every soul, the spirit's young.
The path unfolds, a sacred scroll,
With every step, we find the whole.

When trials test, and fears ignite,
His whispered hope shall shine so bright.
In every tear, a strength to rise,
With holy whispers, we touch the skies.

Embrace the light, let shadows fade,
In faith decayed, new life is made.
For in His love, we find our role,
Guided by whispers, we become whole.

The Serene Glow Within

In quiet hearts, a feeling grows,
A flame of peace, as soft wind blows.
In stillness found, His grace unfolds,
A serene glow, more precious than gold.

Each whispered thought, like morning's dew,
Awakens dreams, so fresh and true.
Through trials faced, His light we share,
The glow within, a loving care.

When storms arise, and shadows loom,
In faith we stand, dispelling gloom.
The heart that shines, reflects His grace,
In every trial, we find our place.

The glowing light, our guiding star,
In every wound, reminders mar.
Yet from the pain, we learn to sow,
With every seed, the love will grow.

So let your heart, be filled with song,
In every step, where love belongs.
Illuminate the world with cheer,
For the serene glow, shall draw us near.

A Light for the Weary Soul

When burdens weigh on weary hearts,
A flicker glows, in darkest parts.
With hands outstretched, He calms the storm,
A light to guide, our souls transform.

In quiet moments, stillness reigns,
A gentle spark, where hope remains.
With every sigh, and every prayer,
We find the light, forever there.

Through darkest nights, His love will shine,
A beacon bright, in every sign.
When paths are lost, and faith runs low,
His light will lead, the way we go.

In every trial, our spirits rise,
With love as fuel, we touch the skies.
For weary souls, in pain confined,
A light burns bright, with love entwined.

So seek that light, let shadows fade,
In every heart, new life is made.
For weary souls, there's peace in store,
A guiding light, forevermore.

The Shimmer of Belief

In twilight's hush, belief takes flight,
A shimmer glows, through darkest night.
With every doubt, a spark ignites,
A dance of faith, our hearts invite.

In trials faced, we stand so tall,
For in His love, we shall not fall.
For hope's embrace, wraps round our soul,
The shimmer bright, makes us whole.

Through valleys deep, where shadows creep,
The light of belief, its vigil keep.
A tender glow, through storms we find,
A guiding love, forever kind.

In every heart, a hymn unfurls,
The shimmer bright, all darkness swirls.
With every breath, we know His grace,
In every moment, we find our place.

So lift your eyes, and boldly see,
The shimmer of true belief shall be.
For in our hearts, the light shall stay,
A guiding flame, our souls display.

A Tapestry of Shining Moments

In every heart, a thread of light,
Woven deep in sacred night.
With prayers spoken, hopes take flight,
A tapestry that shines so bright.

Among the trials, faith does rise,
In whispered truths, the spirit flies.
A journey paved with love's sweet guise,
Each moment cherished, never dies.

Through valleys low, and mountains high,
With humble hearts, we learn to cry.
In grace, we find the reasons why,
As life's great play does pass us by.

Together in a sacred place,
We find our strength, we find our grace.
In every challenge we embrace,
A shining moment we must trace.

And when the shadows gather round,
In love and hope, we stand our ground.
For woven in, the peace is found,
In every soul, a light profound.

The Lullaby of Divine Whispers

In the quiet, soft and sweet,
Divine whispers, our hearts meet.
A lullaby, a gentle greet,
In sacred silence, love's heartbeat.

Night's embrace, the stars awake,
Promises spoken that never break.
With every breath, our spirits quake,
In tranquil peace, we take our stake.

Tender prayers like feathers fall,
A grace that answers every call.
Through darkest hours, we heed the thrall,
In deep surrender, we stand tall.

Soft the hands that cradle night,
Guiding us toward the light.
In every sigh, a hope ignites,
In love's great arms, we take our flight.

The dawn shall come, a golden ray,
With every whisper, we shall stay.
In the stillness, love's ballet,
In every heart, a hymn to play.

Guiding Stars Above

The stars above, a cosmic guide,
Leading souls on love's sweet tide.
In every heart, those lights reside,
With faith as compass, never hide.

Through shadowed paths, our spirits tread,
With every tear, a prayer is said.
In harmony, by hope we're led,
To distant shores where dreams are bred.

Celestial bodies, shining bright,
In darkest hours, they bring us light.
With every wish cast into night,
A promise made, all will be right.

With whispers soft as winds have blown,
In every heartbeat, love is sown.
The guiding stars, forever known,
Together, we shall find our home.

In night's embrace, a truth unspun,
In every journey, we are one.
With targeting stars, we feel the sun,
In sacred light, our hearts are run.

A Warm Glow in the Storm

In the tempest, where shadows play,
A warm glow lights the darkest way.
With tender hands, we learn to stay,
Embraced by love, come what may.

The howling winds may test our heart,
Yet from the storm, we won't depart.
In faith and truth, we find our art,
From whispered vows, new lives shall start.

Through pouring rain, we seek the spark,
In every trial, we leave a mark.
With every beat, igniting the dark,
In unison, we hear the lark.

Together we rise, unbroken souls,
With grace we fill our empty bowls.
In love's embrace, we find our goals,
A beacon bright, that corners roles.

When storms retreat and skies are clear,
A warmth remains, as love draws near.
In every heart, a place to hear,
The glow of hope, forever dear.

Candles of the Lost

In shadows deep, the candles glow,
Illuminating paths we know.
Each flicker tells a tale of woe,
A silent prayer for souls that flow.

The whispers echo through the night,
As flames unite in sacred light.
For every heart that lost its fight,
We light a candle, bold and bright.

In memory, we gather near,
With hopes to soothe each hidden fear.
A beacon shine, our hearts sincere,
In love's embrace, we hold them dear.

Through darkest times, we seek the spark,
Together we ignite the dark.
In unity, we light the arc,
A tribute in the silent park.

With each small flame, a promise made,
That love will linger, never fade.
In this gentle flame, we're not afraid,
The lost are held in light displayed.

Light's Eternal Dance

In twilight's glow, the candles sway,
A dance of light that leads the way.
Each flicker whispers, come what may,
In faith we trust, no disarray.

As shadows stretch against the wall,
We seek the light, we heed the call.
In unity we rise, not fall,
For love is found in every hall.

The flames may flicker, but never die,
A testament to the open sky.
With hearts ablaze, we watch them fly,
In reverence, we lift our cry.

A symphony of light and grace,
In every spark, we find our place.
United hands in soft embrace,
With every flicker, we trace the face.

So let us dance, both near and far,
As candles shine like distant star.
In light's embrace, our spirits are,
Together, we become what we are.

The Comforting Flicker of Faith

In quiet nights, the candles glow,
A gentle warmth, a love we know.
With every flicker, soft and slow,
Our spirits rise, our hearts bestow.

The light embraces fears we hold,
A promise whispered, brave and bold.
In faith's deep warmth, our souls are told,
Of love eternal, bright and gold.

When shadows threaten to ensnare,
The flicker calls us, teaching care.
In darkest times, we find a prayer,
A bond unbroken, always there.

Through trials faced, we light the way,
With every flame, we find our stay.
In the comforting glow, we may,
Rejoice in love, come what may.

Let every candle lead us home,
In flickering faith, we will not roam.
The places lost, we shall not comb,
For love is here, in faith we comb.

Celestial Blooms of Grace

In gardens vast, where candles bloom,
The air is rich, dispelling gloom.
With every light, a gift we groom,
In hearts of faith, there is room.

Each flicker holds a prayer divine,
A sprout of hope, a sacred sign.
In unity, our spirits entwine,
The grace of love, eternally shine.

From every petal, a story unfolds,
Of lives lived bright, a love that holds.
In flickering light, our heart beholds,
The warmth of grace that never folds.

With gentle hands, we tend the flame,
In every heart, there lies a name.
The breath of life, it's not in vain,
The blooms of grace softly remain.

As starlit skies watch over us,
Our flickering faith ignites the trust.
In every candle, love's great thrust,
Celestial blooms, in light we rust.

Footprints in the Light

In the golden dawn, we walk in grace,
Footprints left upon this sacred place.
The path of hope does gently unfold,
Guiding us through the stories told.

With every step, His love shines bright,
Illuminating darkness, dispelling fright.
In trials faced, we find our might,
For in our hearts, He is the Light.

We gather strength in the silent prayer,
Each whispered wish, He hears us there.
In unity, our souls take flight,
Together walking in the light.

Through valleys deep and mountains high,
We trust in His hand, we shall not sigh.
For every shadow speaks His name,
And with each heartbeat, love's the same.

With gratitude, we lift our eyes,
To clouds above and endless skies.
The joy of faith, a gentle song,
In the light of Him, we all belong.

The Glint of Eternal Faith

In the stillness, we find the call,
A glimmering truth that connects us all.
In the sacred grasp of tender grace,
Eternal faith lights every space.

Through trials deep and storms that rage,
We turn the page on every stage.
Faith like a beacon, fierce and bold,
Whispers of love in tales untold.

In moments dark, when hope seems lost,
We stand united, no matter the cost.
For in His arms, we find our way,
Guided by light, come what may.

With hearts ablaze, we share the flame,
Each soul ignited, none are the same.
In harmony, we sing His praise,
Under the sun's kind, warming rays.

Let faith be the glint in our eyes,
Reflecting truth beneath the skies.
In every heart, His spirit thrives,
The glint of faith forever drives.

The Shining Journey Within

Within our hearts, a journey begins,
A shining light where grace always wins.
In silence deep, we hear the sound,
Of love resounding, pure and profound.

With every breath, we draw Him near,
In whispers soft, we know no fear.
For journeys within are sacred rites,
To uncover the truth, ignite the lights.

When shadows graze upon our soul,
His guiding hand makes broken whole.
Through winding paths, we seek the dawn,
In the light of faith, we will carry on.

Embrace the peace that dwells inside,
Let faith be our anchor, love our guide.
In the depths we seek, a world anew,
Shining brightly in all we do.

As we journey forth, hand in hand,
On sacred ground, together we stand.
Illuminated by His pure grace,
In the journey within, we find our place.

The Light of All Horizons

The dawn awakes with whispers sweet,
A light of hope, our hearts repeat.
From distant shores, to skies so wide,
We find the light where dreams abide.

In every corner, His love we trace,
The light of all horizons fills our space.
With every breath, it calls us near,
In the vast expanse, we shed our fear.

Each moment shared, a piece divine,
He paints the world with love's design.
Through valleys low and mountains steep,
In the light of Him, our souls will leap.

With faith unbroken, we rise above,
A journey blessed, wrapped in His love.
In unity, we stand as one,
Warmed by the light of the eternal sun.

So let us wander, hand in hand,
With grateful hearts, we'll make our stand.
In the light of all horizons bright,
We find our home, our endless light.

Seraphic Glows Along the Way

In shadows deep where spirits dwell,
The seraphs sing their sacred swell.
With wings of light, they guide the soul,
Through trials fierce, they make us whole.

A path adorned with radiance bright,
Unfolds with hope, dispelling night.
In every breath, divine embrace,
We find our peace, we seek His face.

The whispers soft, the prayers rise,
To heavens high, beyond the skies.
In every tear, in every prayer,
The seraphs linger, always near.

In gentle winds, their voices call,
Through valleys low, they cover all.
With faith as shield, we brave the fray,
Together in this blessed way.

In moments still, our hearts embark,
Upon the path that lights the dark.
With seraphic glow, we walk anew,
With every step, our vision true.

Illuminations of the Sacred Journey

Beneath the stars, a quest unfolds,
In softest light, the truth beholds.
Each step we take, a tale divine,
In sacred paths, our spirits twine.

The journey long, with burdens shared,
In love's embrace, our hearts prepared.
With grace we walk, through storms we strive,
In every breath, we feel alive.

The light within, a guiding flame,
Illuminates each heart's fair claim.
Through trials faced, we come to see,
The sacred truth that sets us free.

With open arms, we gather near,
In fellowship, dispelling fear.
Together bound by faith's sweet call,
In every rise, we shall not fall.

The steps we take, a dance of grace,
In holy lands, we find our place.
With love as guide, we journey forth,
Towards radiant new dawns of worth.

Heartstrings Touched by Light

In quiet corners, hearts align,
As light descends, they intertwine.
A melody of hope resounds,
In every note, true love abounds.

With whispers pure, the spirits guide,
As heartstrings hum, they turn the tide.
In moments shared, our souls take flight,
Touched by the warmth of endless light.

Each heartbeat marks a sacred time,
In love's embrace, we rise and climb.
With every tear, a joy reborn,
Our hearts, a tapestry adorned.

Through valleys deep and mountains high,
In unity, our voices cry.
The light it weaves, a radiant thread,
Connecting all, both living and dead.

With open hearts, we gather near,
In hope's pure grace, we cast off fear.
As heartstrings touch with celestial fire,
We rise as one, in love's desire.

Ethereal Echoes of Enlightenment

In realms unseen, where silence reigns,
Ethereal echoes break the chains.
With whispered truths, they softly call,
Awakening souls who hear their thrall.

Through paths of thought, we journey deep,
In quietude, the secrets keep.
The gentle wind, a guiding breeze,
Unveils the mysteries, brings us ease.

Each moment blooms, a sacred trust,
In unity, we rise from dust.
With every echo, wisdom flows,
Like rivers wide, the spirit knows.

In stillness found, our hearts align,
Eclipsed by grace, the light divine.
With every thought, the world expands,
In echoes true, the heart understands.

From shadows cast, to brilliance bright,
In every soul, the spark ignites.
Our journey paved by love's embrace,
In ethereal echoes, we find grace.

Unveiling the Hidden Luminescence

In shadows cast by doubt and fear,
A flicker glows, so crystal clear.
Beyond the veil, a truth resides,
With faith, the hidden light abides.

Through trials deep, the spirit learns,
To seek the flame, for wisdom yearns.
Beneath the weight of worldly night,
Awakens hope, a guiding light.

In silence, whispers softly call,
Illuminating one and all.
Grace flows like rivers, pure and wide,
In every heart, the light confides.

With every breath, we rise anew,
In unity, our spirits grew.
Together bound, we stand in peace,
In love's embrace, our fears release.

For in the deep, the lumens flow,
Unveiling paths we ought to know.
With open eyes, the truth we see,
A realm of light, our destiny.

The Heart's Resplendent Glow

From depths of silence, whispers rise,
A tender light beneath the skies.
The heart ignites, a sacred flame,
In every beat, love calls our name.

In moments pure, the spirit sings,
Awakening to the joy it brings.
With every tear, the soul became,
Refined by fire, forever tame.

Let kindness weave a tapestry,
Of laughter, joy, and harmony.
For in the giving, we shall find,
The glow of love, both soft and blind.

As dawn breaks forth, the shadows flee,
Your heart, a mirror, reflecting me.
In unity, our light shall flow,
Together, we shine, the heart's glow.

With every pulse, eternity,
In love's embrace, we are set free.
The heart shall glow, a beacon bright,
A sacred flame, our pure delight.

Songs of Celestial Brilliance

In heavens high, the angels sing,
Notes of grace on gentle wing.
Each melody, a sacred spell,
In echoes pure, our spirits dwell.

With every rise of morning light,
We join the chorus, pure delight.
A symphony of love untold,
In harmony, the brave and bold.

Through trials faced and burdens borne,
The songs of hope are softly worn.
Awakening dreams long kept inside,
In every heart, the stars abide.

Let every voice, in unison,
Proclaim the love that's just begun.
For in each strain, celestial grace,
We find our truth, our sacred place.

As moonlit nights embrace the skies,
We lift our hearts, a bright reprise.
In songs of brilliance, we shall thrive,
Together bound, forever alive.

The Sacred Arc of Light

A radiant arc across the skies,
A bridge of love that never dies.
In stillness found, the spirit soars,
Connecting hearts to heaven's doors.

Within this path, the sacred flows,
Infinite grace, the spirit knows.
Each step we take, a promise kept,
In faith and trust, through pain we've wept.

As whispers dance in twilight's glow,
Awakening souls, our truths bestow.
In every challenge, blessings rise,
A tapestry of unseen ties.

Together, we embrace the light,
Through darkest hours, we find our sight.
The arc directs our way ahead,
With love as guide, no heart should dread.

In every prayer, a spark is found,
A testament to love unbound.
As light unfolds, we walk the path,
In unity, we feel love's wrath.

A Pilgrimage of the Heart

In quiet places, spirits rise,
Guided softly by whispered sighs.
Each step a prayer, a sacred art,
Wandering deep, a pilgrimage of the heart.

Through valleys low and mountains high,
Seeking grace beneath the sky.
With every breath, a promise dear,
To follow love, to walk without fear.

The path unfolds as branches sway,
In the light of dawn, we start our way.
Voices mingle, a hallowed sound,
In every heartbeat, His love is found.

With faith as wings, we rise above,
Embracing the truth, the endless love.
In unity, our souls will thrive,
For in this journey, we come alive.

Eternal whispers guide our feet,
In this venture, life is sweet.
The pilgrimage calls, we heed the start,
With every step, a beat of the heart.

Beneath Heaven's Veil

Underneath the celestial dome,
We find a whisper that feels like home.
Stars align in a cosmic dance,
As we seek the sacred chance.

Beneath heaven's veil, a promise bright,
In shadows deep, we search for light.
With open hands and eager souls,
Together we play our destined roles.

Each prayer like petals, gently cast,
Into the winds, to the future vast.
With every hope, we weave the threads,
In unity, the spirit spreads.

The sky above, a tapestry wide,
Where dreams take root and love abides.
In every heart, a glimmering sign,
That connects us all, a love divine.

With faith as compass, we navigate,
Through the trials that we create.
Beneath heaven's veil, we shall reside,
In grace and mercy, forever tied.

The Spark of Faith

A flicker glows within the dark,
A whisper soft, a gentle spark.
When shadows loom and doubts take flight,
The spark of faith ignites the night.

In every struggle, strength is born,
Through every sorrow, hope is worn.
Like embers glowing in the rain,
The flame of trust shall not be slain.

A beacon bright through life's tempest,
Guiding souls on their humble quest.
In valleys low and mountains steep,
The spark of faith we vow to keep.

As tendrils reach for heaven's grace,
We find our truth in this sacred space.
In every heart that dares to dream,
The spark of faith will always gleam.

So nurture it with love's embrace,
Let kindness bloom, let mercy chase.
For in the fire of the spirit's play,
The spark of faith will light our way.

Chasing Dawn's Embrace

In the quiet hour before the rise,
We seek the warmth, the open skies.
Chasing dawn's embrace, we find our grace,
Awakening hope in every place.

With every heartbeat, a chance reborn,
To dance with light in the early morn.
Each moment cherished, a gift divine,
In the chase for truth, our hearts entwine.

The sun peeks through, with golden rays,
Illuminating all our ways.
In shadows cast, we find our stride,
Chasing dawn's embrace, hope is our guide.

With open arms, we greet the day,
In joy and love, our spirits play.
Through trials faced and fears dismissed,
Chasing dawn's embrace, in faith we persist.

As day unfolds, our journey flows,
In every trial, the heart still knows.
Chasing dawn's embrace, we rise anew,
In every moment, our dreams come true.

Milton Keynes UK
Ingram Content Group UK Ltd.
UKHW020041271124
451585UK00012B/987

9 789916 897195